The Trial of John Lomas and Edith Morrey, for the Wilful Murder of George Morrey, Farmer, at Hankelow, Cheshire, (Master of the said John Lomas, and Husband of the said Edith Morrey,) at the Castle of Chester, on Friday the 21st of August, 1812.

Anonymous

The Making of Modern Law collection of legal archives constitutes a genuine revolution in historical legal research because it opens up a wealth of rare and previously inaccessible sources in legal, constitutional, administrative, political, cultural, intellectual, and social history. This unique collection consists of three extensive archives that provide insight into more than 300 years of American and British history. These collections include:

Legal Treatises, 1800-1926: over 20,000 legal treatises provide a comprehensive collection in legal history, business and economics, politics and government.

Trials, 1600-1926: nearly 10,000 titles reveal the drama of famous, infamous, and obscure courtroom cases in America and the British Empire across three centuries.

Primary Sources, 1620-1926: includes reports, statutes and regulations in American history, including early state codes, municipal ordinances, constitutional conventions and compilations, and law dictionaries.

These archives provide a unique research tool for tracking the development of our modern legal system and how it has affected our culture, government, business – nearly every aspect of our everyday life. For the first time, these high-quality digital scans of original works are available via print-on-demand, making them readily accessible to libraries, students, independent scholars, and readers of all ages.

biblioLife
old books. new life.

JOHN LOMAS.

OF

JOHN LOMAS AND EDITH MORREY

FOR THE

WILFUL MURDER

OF

GEORGE MORREY,

FARMER, AT HANKELOW, CHESHIRE,

(Master of the said John Lomas, and Husband of the said Edith Morrey,)

AT THE CASTLE OF CHESTER,

On Friday the 21[illegible] August, 1812

BEFORE

THE HON. ROBERT DALLAS, HIS MAJESTY'S CHIEF JUSTICE,

AND

THE HON. FRANCIS BURTON, HIS MAJESTY'S OTHER JUSTICE.

ILLUSTRATED WITH

A GROUND PLAN OF MR. MORREY'S HOUSE,

AND OF THE UPPER ROOMS.

TO WHICH IS ADDED,

AN APPENDIX.

CHESTER:

PRINTED BY JOHN MO[illegible]K.

And S[illegible] b[illegible] Mrs. Sn[illegible]son [illegible] Mr. [illegible], Nantwich; Mr. Taylor, Northwich; Mrs. Evans, Knutsford; De[illegible]n and Co. Stockport; Wilson, Macclesfield; Dean, Congleton; Parker, and Jones, Whitchurch; and Mrs. Hurst, Shopkeeper, Middlewich.

1812.

14,

PREFACE.

OF all the crimes of which human depravity is capable, there is none so strongly tinged with the black hue of moral turpitude, as that of deliberate murder! In every country, where we can trace the footsteps of civilization, it is held as the highest species of offence and even the barbarous savage, uninstructed in the page of revelation, and unrestrained by the penalty of human laws beholds it with abhorrence Nor are we left to infer, from the intimate connection there necessarily subsists between the Creator and his creatures, what is the Almighty's estimate of the offence, as he hath expressly declared, that " whosoever sheddeth man's blood by man shall his blood be shed "

It is a subject of wonder, and much more so of painful regret, that in a country like this, where the laws, by affording equal rights to all ranks in the community, protect the humblest individuals from the oppressions of his neighbour, and thereby remove numberless sources of personal animosity, and occasions of revenge, we should have to record such frequent and soul-rending narratives of murders and assassinations! The history of the kingdom, for the last few months, contains recitals of sanguinary barbarity heretofore unknown in this country Within that period, we have seen two whole families, consisting of seven persons, massacred in their own dwellings, and the supposed assassin filling up the measure of his iniquities, by self-destruction! We have witnessed the ruthless hand of an infuriated villain stretched out in the deliberate murder of a minister of state and an exalted nobleman and his lady, the Count and Countess D'Autringue, destroyed together, by a menial servant And lastly, we behold, as will be exhibited in the following pages, a foul, unnatural conspiracy, deliberately formed, and systematically consummated, to deprive an affectionate husband, and an indulgent master, of his life! But we

shall not here pursue the latter transaction further,—one of the criminals has already paid the forfeit of his life to human laws, and we trust has found remission from the penalty of the divine—the same fate awaits the other, and we sincerely hope, that by penitential contrition, she will obtain that mercy from her God, which she refused to her murdered husband!

It may be necessary to apprize the reader, that in taking down the *following trial*, it was not thought necessary to take every question and answer formally and indiscriminately, a method, which would doubtless be objectionable to many, in two particulars, that of rendering it tediously prolix, and swelling the book to an unnecessary extent. At the same time, the publisher of this work deems it necessary to state, that in all cases the substance of the evidence is given, and in *material* points, the questions and answers, as they occurred: and he may also add his hopes, that no serious inaccuracy will be found. For the purpose of compressing the work into as small a compass, and little price as possible, that part of Mr Benson's opening speech, which detailed the evidence he had to produce, has been omitted, as perfectly nugatory, the whole substance of it being contained in the examination of witnesses. For a similar reason, the recapitulation of the evidence, as delivered by the Chief Justice has not been inserted, but the whole of his address to the Jury, not immediately connected with the evidence, as well as his observations on passing sentence, have been most scrupulously preserved, and are accurately detailed.

The sanction of a solemn oath, by which every Juror is bound to an impartial decision, is a satisfactory guarantee to the criminal, of an honest verdict; and the mild spirit and practice of our laws invariably lead to mercy, where any doubt arises. In the present case, however, the evidence was too convincing and conclusive in all its parts, to admit a shadow of doubt, and the verdict, such as could not disturb the peace of the most conscientious and scrupulous. Yet, after all, it must be satisfactory to know, that the evidences of guilt are confirmed by the voluntary confession of the accused party.—The publisher is therefore happy in the opportunity of presenting the public, in this little publication, with two well-authenticated documents, in which the unfortunate malefactors acknowledge their foul guilt, under the sanction of their own signatures. For these, the publisher and the public are indebted to the kindness of two gentlemen who have supplied them for this work; and as they have the acknowledgments of the former, they are entitled also to the thanks of the latter.

The Plan of Mr. Morrey's house, which is inserted immediately before the Appendix, will serve greatly to illustrate some material parts of the evidence. For this also, the publisher is indebted to one of the gentlemen alluded to, and it is presumed it will be found correct. The publisher indulges in the hope that considering the disadvantages of a hasty publication, rendered necessary by the impatience of public curiosity, the pamphlet possesses the main substance of its subject, and all the authentic documents, that can render it interesting.

Chester Courant Office, August 26, 1812.

TRIAL OF

J. LOMAS, and E. MORREY,

FOR MURDER, &c

The King on the prosecution of JAMES MORREY, *against* JOHN LOMAS *and* EDITH MORREY.

THIS trial has excited more general interest throughout the county, than any other we ever remember. The diabolical murder of George Morrey, of Hankelow, in April last, which gave rise to it, must be fresh in the recollection of the public; and whether we advert to the relative connexion between the murdered and the murderers, or to the extreme barbarity of the circumstances attending the murder, it will, thank heaven, there will be found few parallels to it in the history of the most abandoned of wretches. The hand which lifted the murderous instrument was that of his own servant, an inmate, whose protection he had a reasonable claim upon; the heart that conceived this deed of horror, and the person who appears to have encouraged and prompted its execution, that of her who had for many years sustained the character of a wife, and who in that sacred relationship, had brought eight children into the world. The season selected, the hour of midnight, the defenceless period of sleep, at a time too, when, as appeared in evidence, the unsuspecting victim, was in a state of inebriation. The discharge of a pistol, a musket, or the dagger plunged to the heart in a moment, would have been an act of mercy, when compared with the torturing blows of an axe, upon the most sensitive part of the human frame, often repeated, amidst the groans of the extremest anguish. We are compelled to state, that all these aggravations of guilt, this vast accumulation of cruelty met together in this cruel and barbarous murder.

At eight o'clock on the morning of Friday, August 21, the Court met and the jury was impannelled, consisting of the following gentlemen

Edward Gee, Macclesfield,
John Jackson, Stockport,
Charles Turnock, Macclesfield,
Samuel Copeland, Stockport,
Joseph Roe, Macclesfield,
J Broadhurst, Stockport,
Samuel Jepson, ditto,
Charles Swale, ditto,
Matthew Pickford, Adlington,
John Massey, Nether Audley
Samuel Sidebotham, Bredbury,
George Scott, Brennington

Counsel for the Prosecution, Mr Benyon, Attorney-General, and Mr D. F Jones Attorney, Mr F Thomas, Coroner

Counsel for Lomas, Mr Lyon, Attorney, Mr Dicas

For Edith Morrey, Mr Cross and Mr Hill, Attornies, Messrs Edleston and Elwood

On being arraigned, the two prisoners pleaded *Not Guilty*

The indictment charged John Lomas, servant of the late George Morrey with wilfully and traitorously murdering his master on the 12th of April last, and Edith Morrey, his wife with being present at the time of the said murder, and aiding, helping, abetting, assisting, comforting, and maintaining the said John Lomas, in the commission of the same

Mr D F Jones opened the pleadings, and in a speech, distinguished for perspicuity and feeling, Mr Benyon addressed the jury He observed, that a most foul and barbarous murder had been committed on the day stated in the indictment, on the person of the late George Morrey, a farmer, at Hankelow, in this county The learned Gentleman entered generally into the heinous nature of the crime of murder, observing that all civilized nations, as by common consent, invariably visited it with one punishment—that of death But the present case was so marked with every kind and degree of enormity, as to deserve a reprobation above the power of expression It was far from his intention, however, to deprive the prisoners of a fair and dispassionate trial, and he emphatically urged upon the jury, the necessity of banishing every unfavourable impression which might have been created in their minds by common report, and rumour. The constitution had defined their duty to be a decision acderoring only to the evidence of facts He had heard these rumours himself, and indeed the murder of Morrey had been so notorious, and the imputation of guilt had so generally been attached to the prisoners, that it was impossible but the jury had also heard them But he only called upon them for an unbiassed verdict, founded upon testimony the most satisfactory and unsuspected Mr. Benyon then observed, he would shortly state to them the evidence he had to produce, which he proceeded to do, in the clearest manner As the substance of this part of his address, however, will be disclosed in the sequel, we shall proceed to the examination of the witnesses

EVIDENCE

Mr John Groom, Solicitor of Audlem, proved the marriage of George Morrey, with Edith Morrey at Wybunbury in 1797, by producing a copy of their marriage lines, extracted by him from the marriage register of that parish This fact was corroborated by

James Morrey, brother of the deceased, who stated that he was at the wedding-dinner, and that his brother and Edith Morrey's sister were the subscribing witnesses to the marriage

Hannah Evans.—By Mr D F Jones.—She stated she lived with Mr. Morrey at Hankelow in April last, that she knows the prisoner Lomas, who was then her fellow-servant Mr Morrey had five children, that these, with her master and mistress, Lomas and herself, were the whole of the family three of the children slept with her, her bed-room was on the ground-floor, to go to which from the house she must pass through the parlour in which Mr and Mrs. Morrey slept, that none of the children or any other person slept in the room with her master and mistress.—Where did John Lomas sleep? In the room over the back kitchen.—Do the stairs to his room go from the kitchen? Yes.—Did the two other children sleep in Lomas's room?* Yes.—Witness said she did not know the ages of all the children, but the eldest is 13 or 14 She remembers the night of the 11th of April Was you gone to bed that night, when your master came home? No.—About what time did you go to bed? Between twelve and one.—Did you see your master and mistress go to their room? I did.—Was there any alarm or disturbance in the night? Yes, I first heard *two or three blows*.—From what quarter? *From my master's room*.—Did you afterwards hear any noise? Yes, *groaning* I was going

* *The two children who slept with Lomas, were boys, the oldest of whom was from 12 to 13 years of age*

to get through the window.—What prevented you? My mistress pulled me from the window.—Was it dark in the room? No, she had a candle in her hand, and then put it out just when she had opened my door.—What did she say? She told me not to make a noise, for there were murderers in the house.—Was she dressed? She had her under petticoat on.—Did you remain in your room? No, we came out both together, and went into the house.—Was there any desk *(bureau)* in the parlour? Yes.—In going through the parlour did you run against it? Yes.—Did your mistress go against the desk? No, she went round it; the desk was open, and it opened downwards. In going through the room in the dark, must not any person not knowing the desk was open, run against it? Yes, but my mistress did not.—Did you come to the house place? Yes, to light a candle. Witness then stated, that by her Mistress's orders she went up stairs and called up John Lomas; that she called him twice, and he appeared as if he was asleep.—What did you say to him? I told him murderers were in the house; he said I must leave him the candle and he would get up. On which side of the bed did he lie? *The side nearest the door.*—Witness said Lomas came down stairs, that she and he went to call up a neighbour, Betty Spode, and others, who returned with them to the house, but that Lomas observed before they went out his life was in danger by going.—Did you examine the house-floor? Not until the morning, when I saw drops of blood upon it.—Did you trace the blood? Yes, from my Master's room through the house and kitchen to the stair steps leading to John Lomas's bed room.

Cross-examined by Mr. Cross.

She said, when her Mistress came into her room, and afterwards, she was much agitated and frightened.—The front door was only fastened by a loose nail placed over the latch. Did not hear the nail fly out that night. She had been in bed an hour or better when disturbed by the noise.—When her mistress came into the room she was awake. [*Here the prisoner Morrey, without looking at witness, said,* "*No, you were not.*"] She did not tell her mistress of having heard the blows or groans until after she knew her master was killed. Her mistress appeared as much alarmed as witness.—She had lived at Morrey's about a year, and had never seen any unkindness between her Master and Mistress, nor any particular freedom between her Mistress and Lomas. It was about twelve o'clock when her Master came home on the evening of the [illegible]th of April, and was *rather truth [illegible]*. Th[illegible] between [illegible] and Mistress that [illegible] they were [illegible] and [illegible] [illegible] to recollect the [illegible] word of her mistress [illegible] room, but they were [illegible] [illegible] [illegible]

C[illegible]

What time [illegible] [illegible] o'clock [illegible] master [illegible] —Had Lomas had any quarrel with his master [illegible] appeared on good terms.

[illegible] —How long was it after you heard the [illegible], that your m[illegible] came [illegible] room? [illegible] minutes —Did you hear [illegible] screaming, [illegible], or any other person [illegible] I heard no cry, or alarm.

By the [illegible] —[illegible] In the town —Where did you get [illegible] candle [illegible] put out? No, I took one of the [illegible] There [illegible] —Who used to make Lomas's bed [illegible] —Did you then observe any stains of blood upon any part [illegible] —Who washed his linen? Myself and [illegible] you observe any stain upon his shirt? None —[illegible] shirts from your master's? Yes, my [illegible] button holes, Lomas's had but one —In answer to other questions, witness [illegible] her master and mistress never slept with a candle or [illegible] door [illegible] master's room [illegible] the house, [illegible] was fastened by a [illegible] the [illegible], which was [illegible]

THOMAS TIMMIS [illegible]

W[illegible] the next witness, examined [illegible] Mr [illegible] night [illegible] Geo Morrey was murdered [illegible] to him, that on the [illegible] April last, he was called up [illegible] past two o'clock in the morning, by Elizabeth Spode [illegible] in company with John Moors and John Lomas, he went to Morrey's [illegible] that [illegible] entering, [illegible] several minutes observed [illegible] on a chair in the [illegible] with her [illegible] her hand [illegible] her face [illegible] but did not say any thing to [illegible] Moors went into the parlour, where they found the deceased lying upon his face on the floor [illegible] feet near the parlour grate [illegible] the head of an axe under him, the handle of [illegible] bedstead, the room [illegible] very bloody [illegible] did not move him

JOHN [illegible], BY M[illegible]

This witness corroborated the testimony of the [illegible] witness with [illegible] on [illegible] He [illegible] and Timmins on the road [illegible] house, and [illegible] observed, he thought his master [illegible] when [illegible] and witness went into the parlor [illegible] deceased, [illegible] of the prisoners accompanied them On [illegible] into the [illegible], he did examine the corpse [illegible] find the deceased? [illegible] on his belly on the floor —What [illegible] His throat was cut —Did you see an axe? Yes [illegible] against the bedstead —In what state was it? All [illegible] —In what state was the floor? All over blood —In what state were the [illegible] he lay on

By the Court —[illegible] conversation with Mr Morrey? None —Did she quit her chair? [illegible] —Did [illegible] examine whether there were any [illegible] the door or window? Yes, but we found none, it was [illegible] —[illegible] nothing? She said somebody [illegible] at Northwich

[illegible] Hall, by Mr Bennion

This witness gave [illegible] to the two preceeding, relative to the state the deceased was found in Examined the corpse, and perceived a wound on George Morrey's neck it was almost from ear to ear, and very deep —The first time [illegible] was at Morrey's was before day light, and he went thence, [illegible] returned at break of day —Did you observe any thing particular in the house or upon any persons? Yes, I perceived some blood upon the [illegible] of John Lomas —Did you examine the house? I [illegible] was blood on the parlour floor in the house part, on the back [illegible] on the stairs I discovered the *bloody marks of a hand* [illegible] Mr Groom and several others, were with me, I was then sent to take care of Lomas Soon after Mr Groom demanded of Lomas to look into his box Lomas refused saying no constable had a right to look into his box [*This conversation appears to have taken place in Morrey's [illegible]*] He stated, that Mr Groom accompanied by Lomas, and himself, proceeded up stairs to Lomas's room —What did you observe there? When I had got to the top of the stairs, I saw Mrs Morrey at the foot of Lomas's bed, and observed her turn round, after throwing [illegible] I could not see whence she took it, her back was towards me it was some kind of linen, and Mr Groom picked it up —Where did she throw it? Amongst some sacks in the room I saw Mr Groom pick it up from the sacks from the spot where she had thrown it I presently after discovered it was a shirt —In what state was the shirt? The wristbands were quite wet with [illegible] Lomas was [illegible], and on Mr [illegible] I [illegible] was his shirt, he acknowledged it was.—Did you and Lomas [illegible] in the fold? Mr Groom asked [illegible] he had a clean [illegible] Lomas said it was not clean, he had worn it all the week. [*This conversation occurred before the bloody shirt [illegible] his room.*]—Did the shirt appear clean? Quite clean. Mr Groom [illegible] his coat, turned [illegible] sleeves, and I perceived marks of blood upon the [illegible] from the shoulder to the wrist.—Before you went up stairs did you examine the state of the outer door, and did there appear any marks of violence upon it? I did, and no marks of violence appeared.—Did you examine the state of the bureau below stairs, and were there any appearances of violence upon it? I did examine it, and discovered no appearance of violence. Witness did not hear any conversation with Mrs Morrey about the door or bureau, nor any further conversation with Lomas respecting the shirt.—Did you examine the sheets of Lomas's bed, and what were their state? Yes, and I saw two small patches of blood upon them.—Did you see any box in Lomas's room? Yes, upon the bed, beside Mrs Morrey.—Was the lid open? Yes, it was.—Did you see any other article of wearing apparel belonging to Lomas? Yes. Mr Groom brought a waistcoat [illegible] stairs, smeared with blood inside [illegible].—To a question by Mr [illegible], on cross-examination, witness said, Lomas [illegible].—Mr Hill also cross-examined this witness, but nothing of importance was elicited, to weaken his testimony.

By Mr Benyon.—You say the [illegible] you found, was wet? Yes, quite wet.

By a Juryman.—Did any [illegible] of violence appear on the box, as if broke open? No, it appeared to have been opened with a key.

By the Court.—Did Lomas or Mrs Morrey [illegible] the parlour, where the corpse was? No, they remained [illegible]. When you went up stairs to Lomas's room did you find her there? Yes, I did.—Did any person ask her any question? Mr Groom asked her how the murderers had got into the house, and she told him through the front door; she said 150l was gone out of the desk. Mr Groom also asked her if the shirt Lomas had on was the one he wore every day; she said it was not, that it was not a clean shirt.

Mr JOHN GROOM, *Solicitor, Audlem. By Mr D. I. Jones.*

This witness stated he lived at Audlem; that on the morning of the 12th April last, he was called up, and informed of the murder committed at George Morrey's, in Hankelow; that on his way thither, about a mile and a half distant, he endeavoured to find out any suspicious characters, but found none and that [illegible] the house [illegible] in the morning. On your arrival at the house, did you examine whether there were any marks of violence on the [illegible] or on the [illegible] in [illegible] room? I did particularly [illegible] found no appearance of violence.—Describe in what condition you [illegible] the desk. The lid was closed but not locked, the lock [illegible] one of which I found in the desk, the bolt of the lock [illegible]. I tried the screws, and they went in and came out very [illegible] the [illegible] plate into which the lock shot, the lock had not been forced, I found a [illegible] the inside, lying upon some papers, *[illegible]* Did you examine the corpse? Yes, the face was much disfigured [illegible] blood [illegible] there were wounds on the head, and a considerable quantity of blood upon the floor.—When did you first see [illegible] Morrey, and where? Soon after I entered the house I saw her [illegible] before her [illegible].—Did you ask her how the thieves had entered the house? Yes, she told me through the front door, and [illegible] no one speak, but heard a noise in the [illegible] went into the children's room, *(the bed-room of Hannah [illegible])*—Did you see Lomas, and did you observe [illegible] him [illegible] particular? I did, and perceived [illegible] spots of blood [illegible] upon his breeches waistband. I [illegible] shirt; I asked where his dirty shirt was, he said he had it on, he persisted in this, and said he had worn it a week. [illegible] the back door, crossed the [illegible] parlour, where the deceased was, looking [illegible] the deceased to the parlour door [illegible] the kitchen, *whence the stairs lead to Lomas's room, and [illegible] the stairs perceived two or three bloody finger marks.* [illegible] room, in company with Mr Thomas Walker [illegible] the bed, *(the [illegible] in the room)* and discovered [illegible] blood upon them, *on the side next the door*.* There was none on the further side.—Did you see any sack there? Yes, [illegible] yards from the bed.—Did you examine them? I did, particularly.—Did you observe a box? Yes, upon a chest in the same room. I tried to open it but found it locked, there was nothing [illegible]—Where was Lomas at this time? In the yard.—On your way [illegible] yard, did you see Mrs Morrey? I did not. Witness then detailed the circumstances sworn to

* Vide the evidence of Hannah Evans [illegible] that he was on this side of the bed [illegible]

by the last witness, of the stripping of Lomas in the yard, and the discovery of blood upon his coat in the inside —Did the blood appear wet or dry? It was fresh, but rather dry I told Lomas if he would not let me look into his box, I would break it open He then accompanied me and others into his bed-room § Describe what you saw there Ascending the stairs, at the top step, I saw Mrs Morrey, near the bottom of Lomas's bed, with a box in her hand open Was it the same box you had before seen in the room locked? It was the same box I saw her hand in it, and she took something out white with her right hand —What did she do with what she took out? She whirled round her hand, and threw it among some sacks on the opposite side of the room, then turned round towards me and the others who accompanied me, and said, "*Gentlemen here's his box*" † She did not say another word —Were those the same sacks you had before seen?—Yes, they were —Upon searching what did you find? A shirt —In what condition was it? Bloody in the wristbands —Did the blood appear old? No, it was quite wet and fresh, when I touched it, it blooded my fingers —When you say the blood was wet and fresh, could it have been as long on the shirt as from Friday? No, I think not —What followed? I ordered Dooley, the constable, to seize Lomas and upon asking Lomas if this was his shirt, he said it was, nothing was said by the prisoner Morrey I went down stairs, and again asked Lomas concerning the shirt, he repeated it was his I then returned again to the bed-room, and examined more particularly about the sacks, and found a waistcoat, near the place where I had found the shirt It was very bloody both inside and out, and in my opinion, the blood could not be so old as the preceding Friday I took the waistcoat to the yard, (where Lomas was) and asked him if it were his, he said it was —Did you mark the sheets, waistcoat, and shirt you found? I did —Would you know them again?‡ Certainly

Cross-examined by Mr Cross —He could not say whether a knocking at the outside of the front door would not have the effect of shaking out

§ *It does not seem probable that Lomas was aware of his shirt having been locked up in his box, it is most likely it had been secreted there by Mrs Morrey, who it appears had the key of it*

† *Here the prisoner Morrey muttered, in a sulky tone, her face covered with her handkerchief, and her head reclining on the front of the bar, "There is not ten words of truth in what he has said"*

‡ *The awfully disgusting ceremony of producing these bloody-tinged articles to the Court was dispensed with*

the na[illegible] from the latch. If there had been a knocking at the door, might not this noise have been supposed by Hannah Evans, to proceed from her [illegible] room? Yes, it might. He could not say whether the prisoner Morrey had heard of any enquiries having been made for Lomas's box. Witness was sure there was no key in the box when he first saw it, to [illegible] to open it. He tried it with his knife. Lomas could not have been in the room between witness's first and second examination of his box, very few minutes intervening. To a question, whether Edith Morrey had not thrown the bloody shirt on the middle of the room floor, where it might be seen, witness answered she had not.

By Mr. D. F. Jones.—Witness said there was not even a scar upon the [illegible] sure when he first examined Lomas's box, there was no key, on examining it the second time, there was.—Was the linen thrown towards the [illegible]? No, it was thrown from it. On entering the room, I could see the bed, but not the place where the sacks were. The partition between the stairs and room prevented it.

By the Court.—Were the sacks tied? They were.—Are you sure you examined whether there was any thing about the sacks the first time you was in the room? I am sure I did, and there was nothing.—Was the box large enough to contain both the shirt and the waistcoat? Yes, it was. In examining the burean, did you observe whether the articles under the bed were in a state of disorder, as if persons had been rummaging? Every thing appeared in order, and regular.

[illegible] Dooley, Constable of Audlem, Examined by Mr. Bennon.

Witness stated, that on being called early on the morning of Sunday the 12th of April, and hearing, that Morrey had been murdered, he accompanied Mr. Grounds, Thomas Hill, and John Moors, to Morrey's house at Hankelow. After stating generally the circumstances, already given in evidence, witness proceeded, in answer to questions of the counsel, to repeat the conversation he had with Lomas, after the discovery of the bloody shirt [illegible] which was as follows:—That witness asked prisoner if the [illegible] was, and he acknowledged it was. He said he had it on the [illegible], when he bled his master's mare and some calves, and accounted for the blood being upon it by that circumstance. That witness then said, he had contradicted himself for he had before stated, that the [illegible] he had worn a week, upon which Lomas said, "I

1. *The learned Counsel's intention was evidently to render it feasible that the noise occasioned by the murderous blows upon her master's head, might arise from a knocking at the door.*

[illegible] *I [illegible] committed myself, at the [illegible]* —Did you search his pockets? I did, and found a razor sheath. I was present when the pond in the field behind Mr Morrey's house was searched. William Leak picked up a razor and gave it me. Witness then produced the razor with a little blood upon the heel of it, and two hairs upon the edge.—How came you to look into the pond? Lomas told me he had thrown the razor into it. I did not ask him. *In a question by the Court*, how they found the razor in the pond, witness replied, they drew the water off.

[We did not observe the least change in the countenance of Lomas during the exhibition of the razor, with which the barbarous murder was completed. As for H. Morrey, her face could not be seen.]

[At this period of the proceedings the trial had lasted upwards of four hours, and the female prisoner, apparently from excessive heat, seemed faint, and sat down on the bench under the bar. The Chief Justice humanely directed Mr Hudson, the Constable of the Castle, to let the prisoners have some water, or wine, if she preferred it, as well as Lomas. A chair was also offered her, but this she declined accepting, and again stood up at the bar.]

JAMES MORREY, *brother to the deceased, and a farmer at H[illegible]*

Witness says he was called up very early on Sunday morning, about 12, and John Lomas, the prisoner, was one of those who called him. On the road to his brother's, some of them told him, that money had been stolen out of Geo. Morrey's desk, and that he had been murdered. On his arrival at the house, he saw [illegible] Morrey sitting by the fire-side. Did she say any thing to you? She told me her husband had been from home the day before, and that somebody must have followed and murdered him. She informed me the front door had been entered by the nail which fastened the latch dropping out, by the shaking of the door. Witness added, that John Lomas then showed him how the nail would drop out, by putting it over the latch; that when the prisoner shook the door, the nail did fall; that he himself tried the experiment, and found when the nail was put in, the shaking of the door would not move it. Did Mrs Morrey say any thing else to you? Yes, she told me she thought the deceased had been bragging about his money where he had been, and some body had followed him for it. I asked her on which side of the bed she lay, and she told me on the near side. I then enquired, how she escaped? she said when she heard a noise, and that she had run into the children's room.—Did you examine the desk? Not then. I only just looked into it, and saw two shillings lying in it; but the next day I did particularly, and in one of the small drawers I found Geo. Morrey's watch, and a cheque on the Nantwich bank for 120l.

John Bellyse, jun. Surgeon, at Aud[illegible]

Witness stated, that on Monday the 13th April, he examined the corpse of the deceased, that he found an extensive fracture on the left temporal bone of the head, a fracture of the lower jaw, on the left side, a fracture of the bones of the nose, a wound upon the chin and another upon the upper lip, likewise a very extensive wound across his neck, from the centre of his throat to the back of his neck on the right side the incision had divided the muscles of the neck, the windpipe and the jugular vein in length about nine inches, in depth three, and appeared to have been inflicted by some sharp instrument the fractures seemed to be given by some heavy weapon There were also some bruises on his breast bone — Do you think either or both the wounds were such as to produce death? Certainly, the incision on the neck was alone sufficient to produce instantaneous death — Were the fractures such as might have been produced by the head of an axe? They were — Were you not called upon to visit Edith Morrey on Sunday the 12th April? I was — In what state did you find her? I found her lying in a state of insensibility, with her throat cut by some sharp instrument she had lost a great quantity of blood from the wound, which I immediately sewed up Witness also stated, that he visited her on the following morning, Monday. — Had you then any conversation with her? Yes, she informed me, that on the preceding Saturday evening, John Lomas had told her, that the night before, (Friday) he had got up three times to murder his master

Wm Hall, Constable of Hankelow

Witness deposed, that about nine o'clock on Sunday morning, 12th April, he went to the house of the deceased, and saw Edith Morrey — Where did you see her? Sitting by the fire I told her I must take her into custody I sat down upon a chair, and in about five minutes, she dropped upon the floor, and I saw a razor also on the floor, all over blood, I perceived she had made an incision in her throat three inches long and endeavoured to apply something to stop the blood, but she resisted very much, until she was nearly exhausted

By the Court — How happened it, that you did not prevent her from injuring herself? She was sitting in an armed chair, with her head leaning on her left hand, and her elbow resting on the arm of the chair, her apron being wrapped round her left arm, did not see what she was about until she fell

Mr Cross, in cross-examining this witness, was particularly pointed in the question, whether she appeared in her right mind, nothing appeared to witness of the contrary

Wm. Th[illegible]d, Constable of Audlem,

Says he had Edith Morrey in custody on Sunday and Monday, the 12th and 13th April, at the house of the deceased.—Did she say any thing to you during this time? On the morning of Monday she said "I have not been as I should be a great while, but they are bringing me to my senses now, nor I think John (Lomas) has not, for he went moping about at sometimes as if he was not right." She afterwards said, "she wished she had died." I told her she ought to be thankful that the Lord had spared her, when she replied, "The Lord has spared me too long, for he has spared me to suffer, suffer, suffer."—Did she say any thing further? Yes, she said, that on the Saturday evening, John Lomas told her he had got up three times in the night before to murder his master at twelve, one, and half past one o'clock. I asked her why she did not tell her husband, and have Lomas taken up? She said, that John had on Saturday morning gone sulking about, and would not have any breakfast, that she thought he was vexed, and did not care what he said.

By Mr Cross.—When you had this conversation with Mrs Morrey, did she not appear as if she were not in her right mind? I did not perceive any thing of that kind.

Elizabeth Brereton, of Hankelow.

Witness deposed, that on the 12th April she heard George Morrey's house was broken open, that he was murdered, and the house robbed, that about six o'clock the same morning, she went to his house, and asked Edith Morrey how it happened, and she informed witness that there was a noise among the children, and that she ran to them, and while she was there, somebody broke in, killed her husband, and took 150l out of the desk. Witness further said she heard Mr Groom and Mr Walley examine John Lomas about his shirt.—Had you then any further conversation with the prisoner Morrey? Yes, I said to her, "you don't think its Jack, do you?" Mrs Morrey said, "No, I can swear he was asleep in his bed, it is no more him than me; he has blooded himself with bleeding the calves and the mare, and you know it." I answered, the mare was bled at my husband's shop, but I know nothing of the calves.—How long before was the mare bled? Two or three days.—[*This witness's husband is a blacksmith*]—Witness went away from the house, and afterwards returned, when she saw Edith Morrey with her throat cut, and saw Dr Bellyse sew up the wound; that she assisted in putting her to bed, and some time after, she took a chamber-pot from the side of Lomas's bed to empty it, and she perceived some bloody sand at the bottom. Witness further stated, that she sat up with Edith Morrey every other night, ert she was removed to Chester castle, that on a night a short time after the murder was committed, Edith Morres told her, the murder was to have been done the night before, and she would have suffered it, but she would not: that witness asked prisoner, how she knew of it, who answered, Jack had told her so, when Mr. Morres was gone to Nantwich to pay his rent: that Edith Morres also told witness that Lomas got up three times on the Friday night at twelve, one and half past one to kill his master, but hearing him awake, he went to bed again: witness then asked Mrs. Morres why she did not get that young foolish lad taken up: to which prisoner replied, she thought it was nothing but his foolish nonsense, he had ...

... B...ton, of Han...ton,

Swore, that about two months before, he welded a cap on the back part of an axe belonging to George Morres. [Here the fatal weapon was produced in Court: it was an axe with rather an unusual large head, and a remarkably long handle. Marks of dried blood were evidently apparent upon various parts of it, and strong sensations were produced in Court by its exhibition.]—Are you sure this is the same axe you mended for George Morres? I am.

Hannah Evans was again called.

Do you know that axe? (handing it to the witness.) Yes, I do, it was my master's.—When did you see it last, before the murder of your master? I saw it on the night before (Saturday); John Lomas was cutting wood with it.

By Mr B...on.—You said, the blows and groans you heard, appeared to come from your master's room? Yes, they did.

By the Court.—Are you sure you could not mistake any noise the children might make, for what you thought to be blows and groans? I could not.

Here the case on the part of the prosecution closed. No defence was made by Counsel for either of the prisoners: but Mr Cross called several witnesses, who spoke generally of the apparent state of comfort in which the deceased and the prisoner lived together, and of their always having considered her as possessing a humane disposition.

The Chief Justice then read the whole of the evidence, and proceeded as follows:—

"This is the whole of the evidence on the one side, and on the other, and it is for you, now, to compare it with the charge.

The Indictment is for Petit Treason, which, you have been truly told, is an aggravated species of murder, so rendered from the relation in which the prisoners, respectively stood to the deceased, the one being his wife, and the other his servant. But it is necessary I should further tell you, that in the mode of proof, this case differs from a charge of common murder, for in petit treason, as in high treason, two witnesses are necessary to convict. The most positive oath of the most credible witness would not be sufficient. Not however that the law requires two witnesses to the fact of having seen the deceased killed, which in the nature of things can seldom or ever *happen, but one witness to one material* fact, and one to another, each conducing to prove the treason charged, or being, as it is termed, overt acts of that treason, is all required. But this case will not be involved in any incident of such a sort. To go to the what is proved against each prisoner separately, and first, John Jonas.

"He is in the house at the time of the murder committed. At the dawn of day, and two hours after the fact, a spot of blood is seen upon his face—suspicion arises—he is searched—the lining of the sleeves of his coat are found stained with blood—blood is upon the waistband of his breeches—and, at this time, nothing further being discovered, the account he gives is, that it was from the bleeding of his master's calves and mare the Friday before. The shirt which he had on proves to have been one perfectly clean, though on being asked, for his dirty shirt, he asserted it to be such, adding that he had worn it all the week; and as to this, one of the witnesses proves that, having asked him, in the fold, if he had the shirt on when he bled the calves and mare, he said, "the 'shirt he had on he had worn a week, and had it on then,' on which, the witness asked him, 'how he could say he had the dirty 'shirt on when he bled the calves and mare, when he said he had 'had the clean shirt on a week, saying, you have convicted your'self by that—to which the prisoner answered, I have. His pocket was then searched, and in it was found a razor sheath, and, being then asked, what he had done with the razor? he said, he had thrown it into the pond, from which, the water being drawn off, it was there accordingly found, blood being on the heel, and hair on the edge. I need scarcely add, that in his room, a box, which he had refused to suffer to be searched, were, afterwards, found, under the circumstances I shall presently state, his shirt and waistcoat, drenched with blood, and so fresh as to adhere to the hand of the witness who touched it, to make the trial.

"Such a case, as to him, shuts out all possibility of doubt.

"The next consideration is, as to the other prisoner, Edith Morrey.

"It was Saturday night, or rather Sunday morning, for the family went to bed at near one. It consisted of Mr. and Mrs. Morrey, the five children, Lomas, and the maid-servant. At half-past one, as nearly as she could guess, the latter heard blows and groans, the sound coming from her master's apartment, and jumped up in a state of alarm, to escape by the window. At this moment, her mistress, with only her under petticoat on, entered the room. The account this prisoner wishes to have believed is, that having heard a noise herself, she thought it proceeded from the children who slept in this room—she had entered the room, or rather was entering it, with a lighted candle in her hand—and what is the first thing she does? precisely the last that any mother would have done—wetting her finger and thumb, she puts out the candle, and without asking a single question about the children, she tells the girl, there are thieves or murderers in the house, and pulling her back from the window, prevents her making her escape. The next circumstance is no less singular. She sends Lomas and the maid to the nearest house to give the alarm, and without fear or apprehension, remains alone and unprotected in the house, in which, or about which, the thieves or murderers were supposed to be. When the neighbours arrived, how does she conduct herself? She does not appear ever to have gone near the apartment of her dying, or dead husband—but, being left alone for a few moments—she is caught in the room in which Lomas slept, with her hand in that box which had been locked when examined before, with the bloody shirt of Lomas in her hand, in the very act of throwing it behind some sacks, where it was most likely to remain concealed—and afterwards behind these sacks, is found the bloody waistcoat, which had not been there on the former examination. She is shortly after told she must be taken into custody—with a concealed razor she cuts her throat and drops, all but lifeless on the floor. The next day the surgeon tells you, and the same sort of conversation is proved by other witnesses, she said, that on the Saturday night, Lomas had informed her he had been up three times the preceding night, with an intention to murder her husband, and yet, after the murder had taken place, she declares Lomas is perfectly innocent, and she is sure he was in bed at the time. The excuse attempted to be given to this is, that these were declarations made in a state of distraction—but call it by what name you will, distraction or despair, arising from the consciousness of guilt, or detection, or put it out of the proof altogether—the question will be whether, under any consideration of this case, you can entertain a conscientious doubt of her guilt? If you can, give her the benefit of it; but if not, be the consequences what they may, you will upon this, as upon every former occasion, faithfully perform your duty, and declare your opinion such as it is.—Are then either or both of the prisoners guilty or not guilty of the crime imputed to them?—And in answering this question, without attending to my observations, except as they coincide with your own judgment, let the verdict be entirely your own."

The Jury did not retire from the box, but after a consultation of little more than a minute, returned a verdict against both the prisoners, of—GUILTY.

On the prisoners being asked what they had to say, why sentence of death should not be passed upon them, Judith Morrey, made to Mr Hudson, a short statement, which was by him repeated to the Court—"That Hannah Evans has not spoken the truth; that she did not offer to escape through the window until she (the prisoner) had been two or three minutes in her room; that then she asked Hannah Evans to accompany her to the house, but she would not, until she pushed, or forced her out of the room."

The Chief Justice passed sentence upon the prisoners in the following words:

"*Prisoners at the Bar*,

"You have been convicted of one of the most shocking murders

D

recorded in the annals of human guilt, magnified by the relation in which you, respectively stood to the deceased, into the crime of Petit Treason, that is, Murder of the most aggravated description, and I feel it right to add, you have been convicted by the clearest and most convincing evidence.

"On the general nature of your offence, or the particular circumstances attending it, it is scarcely necessary for me to observe. It is sufficient to have heard them once, and, when the claims of public justice shall be satisfied, I have only to wish for the honor of human nature that we could forget them for ever. With respect to you, John Lomas, I think it proper however to remark, that if in such incalculable guilt, there can be any thing like shades and degrees, though yours was the hand that wielded the deadly axe, and afterwards applied the fatal blade—tremendous as such criminality undoubtedly is, there still is reason to believe, you were the least criminal of the two. For, if in the heart of another, was hatched the murderous mischief—if that heart was lodged in the bosom of a woman—if she stood to you in the relation of superior to servant, and I grieve to have occasion to add, of seducer to the seduced—if the deceased was to her an affectionate husband, and the fond father of her many children—compared with such an offender,—barbarous as you have been—who will not feel something like a tendency to compassion and commiseration for your case. If, further—but I forbear—nor will I pursue into their dreadful detail the particularities of this night of horror. It can be no part of judicial duty, when not rendered necessary for the sake of others, to torture the feelings of the most guilty, in a moment like this, and therefore to you Edith Morrey, I shall not address, personally, any peculiar or appropriate observation. You have heard what I have said to the other prisoner, and your conscience will make the application.—It only remains for me to pronounce the judgment of the law, which is, "That you both be "taken from hence to the prison from whence you came, and that "you be taken from thence, on Monday next, the twenty-fourth "day of August, instant, to the place of execution, and that you "be there hanged by the neck till your bodies be dead, and that "your bodies, when dead, be taken down and be dissected and "anatomized, and the Lord have mercy on your souls."

Immediately after sentence was pronounced Lomas said "I deserve it (the sentence) and [illegible] to [illegible] mercy."*

Edith Morrey's Counsel having intimated that she was pregnant, the officer of the Court addressed her as follows:

"Edith Morrey, what have you to say that execution should be stayed?" The prisoner pleaded pregnancy.

By the Court.—Let a jury of matrons be impannelled.

By the Sheriff.—Let the doors of the Court be closed.

A jury of matrons were then summoned from the ladies in Court, who being sworn retired with the prisoner into the interior of the castle, and after an absence of about a quarter of an hour, returned to the Court with a verdict—*That Edith Morrey was quick with child!*

RECAPITULATION

Of the evidence of guilt against the two prisoners.

AGAINST JOHN LOMAS.

1. The traces of blood from Mr. Morrey's bed-room along the floor, to and upon the stairs leading to his bed room, and the blood upon his sheets.
2. The blood upon his nose and wrist, and also on the lining of his coat sleeves, and on other parts of his dress.
3. His having a clean shirt on by two o'clock on the Sunday morning, and saying he had worn it a week, and his afterwards contradicting that statement, when the bloody shirt was produced, by saying he had the latter on the Friday before when he [illegible] the calves and mare, and by his admitting, on the contradiction being pointed out to him, that he had convicted himself.
4. Edith Morrey being seen to take out of his box in which he kept his clothes, the bloody shirt and waistcoat, which he immediately on their being produced owned to be his, and the waistcoat being the same he wore when he went to bed on the night before the murder.
5. The empty razor case found in his coat pocket, and his acknowledging

* Some persons near Lomas, understood him to say, "*I do not deserve it*," referring his words to the concluding sentence of the judge *the Lord have mercy upon your souls.* But we have since ascertained his words and his meaning to be as we have stated them.

having thrown the razor into an adjoining pond, where it was afterwards found bloody.

6. His being seen using the axe, which was afterwards found in the room of the deceased, on the preceding evening.

AGAINST EDITH MORREY.

1. Her coming with her under-petticoat on, and a lighted candle in her hand, from her husband's room into that of the servant, immediately after the servant's hearing the blows given, and the groans.
2. Her putting the candle out on her entering the servant's room, and preventing her escaping through the window to give the alarm, although she had said there were murderers in the house.
3. The manifest contradiction there is in the story she first told the servant woman, and that which she told afterwards: to the servant she stated that there were murderers in the house, but when questioned afterwards, she stated she heard a noise in the house, and thinking it was among the children in the next room, she got up, and while there, heard some blows struck in her husband's room. It must be observed, Hannah Evans heard the blows before E. Morrey came into the room.
4. The representation which Edith Morrey made, that the desk had been robbed of 150l. and that the robbers came through the front door, in refutation of which, it appeared, that though the front door was found open, and the desk lid down, no violence had been offered to either, and on examination of the contents of the desk afterwards, Mr. Morrey's watch, and a cheque on the Nantwich bank was found undisturbed, in one of the drawers.
5. Mr. Groom having insisted on looking into John Lomas's box in his bed-room, she is found there soon after, with the box, which he had just before left locked, open in her hand, and was seen in the act of hastily throwing something white among the sacks, which proved to be his bloody shirt and waistcoat.
6. Her endeavouring to exculpate John Lomas, when separately questioned by Elizabeth Brereton, and William Dooley, on account of the blood upon his shirt, by saying she could swear he was asleep.
7. Her cutting her own throat with a razor, immediately after being told she must be taken into custody, and by endeavouring to resist every application to stop the effusion of the blood.
8. After being in custody, her stating to different persons at different times, that John Lomas had told her he had risen three on the pre-

ceding night to kill his master: there was a time that she had a complete knowledge of his sanguinary intention, and upon several occasions afterwards harbouring him in the house, and making no discovery of it to her husband.

This important trial occupied the Court from eight o'clock in the morning till two in the afternoon. The court was uncommonly crowded, and the heat was extreme. Edith Morrey, the female prisoner, when first brought into the bar, had a veil before her face, but was ordered to be taken off. She covered her face during the whole of the trial with her handkerchief, and most of the time reclined her head on the front of the bar. She did not appear to be at all affected, and through the whole of the awful process she preserved a sullen unmoved calmness in every part of it. We understand, during her examination of the witnesses, she shed tears. She does not appear, from the time of her imprisonment, to have entertained any apprehensions of being convicted. The week before, it seems, she purchased some articles of wearing apparel, washed up her clothes, and spoke confidently of going home as on the following Saturday.

Lomas was the very counterpart of his fellow prisoner.—From his first being taken into custody, to the period of trial, he openly and unreservedly confessed the crime in all its circumstances; in the exercises of devotion he has been incessantly diligent, said he was perfectly prepared to meet his awful fate, and repeatedly expressed his confidence in the mercy of him, who hath said, '*All manner of sin and blasphemy shall be forgiven unto men.*' This preparedness of mind accounts satisfactorily in our view for the absence of those emotions during his trial, which such a situation in one [illegible] is calculated to excite. Indeed, the fountain of his tears seemed to be dried up. There appeared a fortitude in him which might be taken for insensibility, but which does not deserve such a name, and which we trust, was inspired by the hopes of a better world.

EXECUTION OF LOMAS.

On Monday, August 21, the above unfortunate young man was executed at the East front of the New City Gaol, Chester. He was conveyed from the Castle about twelve o'clock, and supported by two Constables, walked to the boundary of the City, where he was received by the City Sheriffs and placed in a cart which was in waiting. On his being put into the cart the unhappy youth fell upon his knees in which posture he continued, passing along Castle-street, Bridge street, and Watergate-street until he arrived at the New Gaol. In the course of less than half an hour he appeared on the drop in the view of a larger concourse of spectators than ever we witnessed upon any similar occasion. He was attended by the Rev. Mr. [illegible], Chaplain to the county gaol, who, in the forenoon, had administered to him the ordinance of the sacrament, and appeared particularly attentive to his situation. The young man has all along expressed a desire rather to die than live, and indeed every part of his deportment evinced the sincerity of his contrition. He was dressed in a blue coat, [illegible] waistcoat, and light corded breeches, and looked remarkably clean. He appeared particularly fervent in his devotions upon the scaffold, kneeling while the chaplain performed the solemn offices of prayer. When the rope was placed around his neck, he addressed some words to the surrounding multitude, observing he had made his peace with God, and warned them to take example by his present awful situation. Just before the cap was drawn over his face, he saluted the executioner, and when every necessary adjustment had taken place, he gave the signal by dropping his handkerchief, the platform fell, and he was launched into an awful eternity. After the dropping of the floor, he struggled rather violently, but in a few minutes, he was dead.

On the day of execution, Lomas was near three hours with the Ordinary in Mr. Hudson's parlour. He understood that he was to be taken to the city gaol, at twelve o'clock, and during the last half hour was extremely impatient for the arrival of the cart. At the city gaol, when the Ordinary had prayed with him for a few minutes, he raised up his head and said, "I'd like to be going." He was then prepared in the usual way for the drop, where, while the last commendatory prayer was reading, he again expressed himself as before, "I'd like to be going." The handkerchief which he wore about his neck, he requested might be given to Francis Holston, one of his companions in the yard at the castle, who had been very kind and attentive to him during his confinement there.

Lomas was in the [illegible]th year of his age, and has a father and mother living; his grey-headed, afflicted father was in court during some part of his trial. He was rather low in stature, of a fair complexion, and had something prepossessing in his countenance.

PLAN OF MR. MORREY's HOUSE.

GROUND FLOOR

UPPER ROOMS

REFERENCES

A Front Door
B House Place
C Door into Mr Morrey's [illegible]
D Mr Morrey's Bed-room
E His Bed
F Desk or Bureau in the [illegible]
  f desk lid [illegible]
G Door into the Room in [illegible] Hannah Evans, the Servant Maid, [illegible]
H Hannah Evans's Bed-room
I Bed where she slept
K Window, out of which Hannah Evans attempted to escape
L Door into the back Kitchen
M Back Kitchen
N Stairs leading to John Lomas's Bed room
O A long Table
P Fire-grate in Mr Morrey's Bed-room

REFERENCES

A Top of Stairs to John Lomas's Bed-room
  c c Partition at the top of the stairs
B Door into Lomas's Room
C Lomas's Bed-room over Back Kitchen
D Lomas's Bed
E A long Chest in the Room, on which John Lomas's Box stood
F The Box in which Lomas kept his Clothes
G The Sacks on which Edith Morrey threw Lomas's Bloody Shirt and Waistcoat
a Room over House Place
b Room over Mr Morrey's Bed-room

APPENDIX.

The Voluntary Confession of John Lomas,

Of Hankelow, in the County of Chester, [illegible] Servant of George M[illegible], [illegible] Thomas, one of his Majesty's Coroners for the said County, the 11th day of April, 1812, at H[illegible],

WHO SAITH AS F[illegible] —

THAT his Mistress, E[illegible] [illegible] to [illegible] his master, and he was to have [illegible]. She [illegible] him to go to William Shaw's, a public-house in Hankelow, [illegible] afternoon, the 11th of April, to get some [illegible] things ready to kill him. His master was gone to [illegible], and she told him (John Lomas) that he must not go to bed. He [illegible] about 12 o'clock, and as soon as his master was [illegible] asleep, his mistress came up to his room. He was asleep [illegible] kened him, and told him his master [illegible] fast asleep, and he must come and kill him. He [illegible] she [illegible] afterwards came up again, and went down again, and he (John Lomas) followed her. She had got the axe [illegible] and gave it him into his hand. He said it would be found out, and they should be sure to be hanged. She said she would see [illegible] when he was fast asleep in bed, and would send the servant [illegible] to [illegible] up. He (John Lomas) said, his master would [illegible] bed, and she said she would go [illegible] up when he was fast asleep for him to come in [illegible]. She put her hand up two or three times, and [illegible] come in. He (John Lomas) then went in, and his mistress [illegible], held the candle, while he struck his master three times with the axe head. He struck him the first time over his temple. After he had struck him three times, he heard the servant wench, who slept in the next room, get upon the floor, and he said, the servant woman was coming, on which his mistress wetted her finger and thumb and put the candle out. He (John Lomas) ran away towards the door and his master was shouting, "Oh! Lord!" His mistress turned him back again and said he must go again, as he had not killed him, she said he must kill him. Then he went again and struck at him in the dark three or four times, with the axe: he thinks he only hit him once with the head of it, and then he ran out of the parlour. His mistress met him in the house-place, and opening a sheath, took out a razor, which she put into his hand, saying, he must go and kill him out—he must cut his throat. He refused, but she gave him a bit of a push, and said he must go. She then went first, and he followed her with the razor in his hand. She flung the out-door of the house open, and then went into the parlour where the servant girl slept, and shut the door after her, and he (John Lomas) went into the parlour. His master was coming off the bed backwards and he touched him, on which his master rose up and catched at him by the breast and by his right hand that he had the razor in. He (John Lomas) pulled out of his arms, and then laid hold of him by the head, as he was then upon his knees, and cut his throat twice. He loosed him and ran, and his master fell to the floor, and he went up stairs, and got into bed. After a while, the servant girl, Hannah Evans, came up to him to shout him up. She came and shook him, and he desired her to go down stairs again, and to leave the candle. He had the bloody shirt on and did not put his arm out of bed, he was afraid of her seeing it. He then got up and put his coat on over his bloody shirt, he dried his bloody hands upon his waistcoat, he also put his smock frock on, and went down stairs. When he came down stairs, the servant girl said some body had murdered her master and he was desired to go in, and see if he was dead. He went to the parlour door, and just peeped in, and said he thought he was. His mistress desired them to call Betty Spode up, and he and the servant wench went ar shouted her up, and she came with John Moors, James Sandilance, and Thomas Timmis They went in to look at his master, but he did not go in Thomas Timmis came out again, and John Moors went in with the candle He came out again, and they all went to call up Mr James Morrey his master's brother, and he returned with them back again bringing Thomas Hall and Joseph Penlington with him They went into the parlour He (John Lomas) and Thomas Timmis sat in the house They came out again and asked him (John Lomas) to hunt some bags to lay him upon He went up stairs to his own bed-chamber and brought down the winnow sheet and gave it them John Moors and Thomas Hall, went away to search lodging houses, and they came back again with Mr Groom, Mr Dooley and other persons John Moors came into the house for a pair of scissars He (John Lomas) gave him one, and he saw Mr Groom and Mr Dooley measuring the feet in the garden, and he thinks Mr Groom asked him for his shoe He fetched it, and they measured it Mr Dooley and Wm Hall came to him, and said they had some suspicion that he had been concerned in the business He said he had not They said he had, and asked him what made his smock bloody He said he had been bleeding some calves, and the mare They asked him where his dirty shirt was He said that was it he had on Mr Walley said it did not look like a dirty shirt but he stuck to it They said he must strip He pulled off his coat, and they turned his sleeves There was some blood upon the sleeves, and on a button on his breeches Mr Groom came down the stairs, and asked him whether his box was not locked He said it was, and he asked him to give him the key He refused, and Mr Groom said he would break it open He (John Lomas) then went up stairs with others, and his mistress was conveying the bloody things off out of the box She was getting them away He says, when he first put them off, he left them on the floor, and when he went up stairs again he put them into the box and locked it He says when he went from murdering his master it was dark, and he had cut his own right hand, and his hands were bloody with his master's blood. He put his hand in the dark on the table at the bottom of the stairs leading to his room, which left a mark of three bloody fin-

[illegible] He also put his hand upon the stairs which left a mark of [illegible] there. He washed the mark on the table with some [illegible] upon it, and spit on the stairs, and rubbed it off with his feet and his hands.

his
JOHN ✓ LOMAS,
Mark

The before written Confession, was made by the said John Lomas, the day, year and at the place therein first above mentioned, before me

FAITHFUL THOMAS, Coroner.

PARTICULARS

OF A

CONVERSATION

[illegible]

JOHN LOMAS, after his conviction, having expressed a desire to Mr Hudson to see Edith Morrey before he died, Mr H. allowed them in his presence an interview of a few minutes. About 5 o'clock on Sunday afternoon, Lomas was called into Mr Hudson's office a minute or two before Mrs Morrey, and told, by Mr Hudson, that the wretched woman had confessed her guilt; to which Lomas replied, "It is better that she has confessed;" and Mr Hudson observing that it was his wish, as he had spoken to Mr Fish, the chaplain, upon the propriety of it, to let them receive the sacrament together, it appeared to give a degree of satisfaction to Lomas, who said, "I had rather she would receive the sacrament with me."

Mrs Morrey was then brought into the office, and upon seeing Lomas, exclaimed, "Oh! dear!" sat down, and remained in silent affliction for some time, with her face covered—Lomas, who was seated at some distance, endeavoured to comfort and soothe her, telling her to bear up, and to pray for mercy and forgiveness—their sins, he said, were very great, but God was good, and he hoped he would forgive them—he had repented, and he trusted through grace to find mercy. He said, "I must go now, you will have to stay a little longer, all our time is short, and if we repent of our sins we may meet in heaven." He then asked his mistress whether she had ever said to any one, that he (Lomas) had got up to murder his master, at 12, 1, and half-past one, the night before the murder, which she denied—saying, "It is not true they have made that amongst them." She complained of a woman, whom she alluded to, as concerned in the fabrication of such report as one that was never sober—Lomas then prayed to God to forgive them, and to forgive him, for he had done a very wicked act, and he deserved to die for it—He would not wish to live. "If they had not found me guilty, they would not have *done* me justice; it is only doing me justice to hang me. There is a *good* God above and I hope to see my master in the other world." At this Mrs Morrey said, "Pray God you may." Lomas again admonished his mistress, as she had a longer time allowed her, *to confess her sins and repent*. To a question put by Mr Hudson, Mrs Morrey denied that she took the candle into the other room, and said, she would not let the servant girl go through the window—she repeated she did not hold the candle—Lomas said, "Mistress, do not say so; it will do you no good to deny it; when I told you Hannah was coming, you pinched the candle out." Mrs Morrey's reply to this was, "My good lad it was not so, there have been a many false things said;" and she then proceeded to animadvert upon some parts of the evidence upon the trial, which were afterwards by the explanation of Mr Hudson, reconciled and understood by the convicts to be correctly given. Mrs Morrey admitted that she took the shirt out of the box and threw it upon the heap of barley, and Lomas said he put the box upon the bed. When Mr Hudson asked Mrs. M how she could ever expect to be acquitted, she declared it to be from a supposition that Lomas's confession could not be admitted evidence against her. Lomas observed that he was *not likely to do otherwise* than confess—but the confession did not come against them, there was enough, he said, without it. Mrs Morrey then said, her husband had declared the night of the murder, that he should turn Lomas away that week, for he *suspected that he* got up in the night to get to the drink. This, Lomas *said*, was very unlikely, for he had said nothing to him, but appeared very well satisfied, and was joking and in good humour with him that very night. They never had, he said, many hasty words, any thing of that sort was soon over, *they* neither of them ever bore any malice, he liked his *master*, he was a very good master; but, added Lomas, "I wish he had turned me away that night." And

Mrs Morrey repeated, "I [illegible] he had—but I hope you [illegible] be forgiven, and more too—[illegible] as your own fault, you were [illegible] poking at me, and would not let me alone." This was reported [illegible] her by Lomas, who said it was her that would never let him [illegible] and he reminded her of [illegible] an instance of the very [illegible] murder, when she got out of bed and came to him, and [illegible] her to go to bed again, and not do it, and she would not [illegible] was all in a tremble. She replied, "I know I have been to blame as well as you."

Mr Hudson asked whether she could have expected to live happily in case she had been acquitted, and she said she should never have been happy—"I know I have done wrong, and I have sinned." She reminded Lomas of a time when he came back from the coal pit and wanted to have done the deed, and she refused, because he had been bad, and had not eaten any thing, and was weak.

Mr Hudson asked Lomas, how he got the axe that he struck his master with, and he said, his mistress gave it into his hand. The observation he made to this was, "My dear lad, was it not on the chair?" He said, "Why, Mistress, you put it into my hand," which she did not deny, and being asked about the razor, he said his mistress concealed it under her petticoats on her belly—that he took the axe, and whilst his mistress held the candle, he struck his master three times; she then pinched the candle out, and they then both ran into the house-place, where they heard him *groan*, upon which his mistress said, "John, he is alive; go, and kill him." Mrs Morrey, to this, replied, she only made the observation, "John, he is alive!"—he then went and struck him with the axe in the dark, two or three times, and returned, and she gave him the razor, when they heard him still groaning; but Lomas persisted in it before her, that she directed him to go and kill him—to go and cut his throat! She continued to deny this part, whilst he repeated it as true, and he said he did go in consequence, and found his master raised in his bed, and attempting to get off backwards; when getting close up to him, his master appearing to know him, laid his head upon Lomas's breast, and caught hold of Lomas's shirt with his right hand; but Lomas said he thrust his hand away, and got his master's head under his left arm, and cut his throat twice, des-

[illegible] deep, and then run a [illegible] The [illegible] he put under a [illegible] and [illegible] he [illegible], he [illegible] into the pit near the house, [illegible] water [illegible]

Mrs Mo[illegible] by Mr Hud[illegible] about the *truth* of [illegible] declaration, and whether it was [illegible] nearly the truth—and [illegible] said, [illegible] *true*

She said she [illegible] weeks [illegible] with child and entered into a calculation from the time of her being in prison—Lomas asked her about the time of her miscarriage, and she gave him the particular time, stating, that it was the day [illegible] to go to Knighton [illegible] which he seemed to [illegible]

Mr Hudson asked her how long she had been in bed with her husband before she got up to perpetrate the murder but she could not particularly state He questioned her, as to whether her husband was sober, and she said he was sober enough

Mr Hudson then addressed them in the language of admonition and prepared them for a final separation Lomas said, "I "forgive her, but it seems she does not forgive me"—[illegible] said, "I have forgiven every body, and every thing that has been "done against me" Lomas said his half-brother had cursed him (Mrs Morrey) but he said nothing He said nothing [illegible] so much as to see his poor father what grief he was [illegible]—it was a hard case, he said for him to bring children up to this end "God help him, and God help my master's children, I hope they "will take good ways" He then enquired as to what situations they were in, and was informed by his mistress He said his own mother was a very wicked woman Then addressing himself to his mistress he earnestly, and piously called upon her to make her peace with God, and to read the Scriptures and pray "Till I "came," he said, "to this place, I knew nothing of Scripture. "I have been made to read the Bible, and to pray, and am better "off I like the New Testament I have read it, and know that "Christ came down to die for us poor miserable sinners Mis-"tress, I wish well to you, I will leave you a good book of Prayers, "and I hope you will read it" Mrs Morrey said she freely forgave

Lomas, and he said to [illegible] grave her—and finally said fare you well, mistress.

Acknowledged to be true, 24th Aug. 1812, 8 o'Clock, a.m.

The ✓ mark of
JOHN LOMAS
her
EDITH ✓ MORREY,
mark.

Witness,
MATTHEW HUDSON,
J. LLOYD.

PRINTED AND PUBLISHED BY J. MO[illegible]X.

Lightning Source UK Ltd.
Milton Keynes UK
UKOW021804090413

208965UK00007B/490/P